IT'S TIME TO EAT MANGO

It's Time to Eat MANGO

Walter the Educator

Silent King Books
A WhichHead Entertainment Imprint

Copyright © 2024 by Walter the Educator

All rights reserved. No part of this book may be reproduced in any manner whatsoever without written per- mission except in the case of brief quotations embodied in critical articles and reviews.

First Printing, 2024

Disclaimer

This book is a literary work; the story is not about specific persons, locations, situations, and/or circumstances unless mentioned in a historical context. Any resemblance to real persons, locations, situations, and/or circumstances is coincidental. This book is for entertainment and informational purposes only. The author and publisher offer this information without warranties expressed or implied. No matter the grounds, neither the author nor the publisher will be accountable for any losses, injuries, or other damages caused by the reader's use of this book. The use of this book acknowledges an understanding and acceptance of this disclaimer.

It's Time to Eat MANGO is a collectible early learning book by Walter the Educator suitable for all ages belonging to Walter the Educator's Time to Eat Book Series. Collect more books at WaltertheEducator.com

USE THE EXTRA SPACE TO TAKE NOTES AND DOCUMENT YOUR MEMORIES

MANGO

It's time to eat, the mango's here,

It's Time to Eat

Mango

A juicy fruit we all hold dear!

Yellow, red, or green so bright,

A mango snack feels just right.

Pick it fresh, or find it ripe,

Its soft, sweet taste is pure delight.

Peel the skin, so smooth and thin,

A fruity feast will soon begin!

Slice it long, or dice it small,

Mango's flavor will please us all.

Its golden flesh is soft and sweet,

A tropical treat that can't be beat!

Hold a slice and take a bite,

The juicy taste is sheer delight.

It drips and dribbles, but that's okay,

Mango makes a happy day!

It's Time to Eat

Mango

Inside the fruit, there hides a seed,

A little core you'll never need.

Toss it out, and save the rest,

The mango's goodness is the best!

In smoothies, salads, or on a plate,

Mango's flavor is simply great.

Eat it fresh, or make it sweet,

A mango's magic is hard to beat.

It grows on trees, so tall and green,

A mango grove is a lovely scene.

In the sun, they ripen with care,

Nature's gift for us to share.

Share it with your family,

Mango love is pure and free.

Pass it 'round, one slice or two,

It's Time to Eat

Mango

It's mango time for me and you!

Feel the sunshine in each bite,

A mango's joy is pure delight.

Its taste is like a summer breeze,

Mango makes you feel at ease.

So let's all cheer, it's time to eat,

A mango snack can't be beat!

Enjoy the fruit, both young and old,

It's Time to Eat

Mango

The mango's story is sweet and bold!

ABOUT THE CREATOR

Walter the Educator is one of the pseudonyms for Walter Anderson. Formally educated in Chemistry, Business, and Education, he is an educator, an author, a diverse entrepreneur, and he is the son of a disabled war veteran. "Walter the Educator" shares his time between educating and creating. He holds interests and owns several creative projects that entertain, enlighten, enhance, and educate, hoping to inspire and motivate you. Follow, find new works, and stay up to date with Walter the Educator™

at WaltertheEducator.com

www.ingramcontent.com/pod-product-compliance
Lightning Source LLC
LaVergne TN
LVHW052013060526
838201LV00059B/4008